MAKING **SCIENCE** WORK

Music

Heinemann

Julian Rowe

First published in Great Britain by Heinemann Library
Halley Court, Jordan Hill, Oxford OX2 8EJ
a division of Reed Educational and Professional Publishing Ltd

OXFORD FLORENCE PRAGUE MADRID ATHENS
MELBOURNE AUCKLAND KUALA LUMPUR SINGAPORE TOKYO
IBADAN NAIROBI KAMPALA JOHANNESBURG GABORONE
PORTSMOUTH NH CHICAGO MEXICO CITY SAO PAULO

Designed by **AMR**
Illustrations by Art Construction
Originated in the UK by Dot Gradations Ltd, Wickford
Printed in the UK by Jarrold Printing Ltd, Thetford

00 01 99 98 97
10 9 8 7 6 5 4 3 3 2 1

ISBN 0 431 06450 4

British Library Cataloguing in Publication Data
Rowe, Julian
    Music. – (Making science work)
    1. Music and science – Juvenile literature
    I. Title
    781.2

Acknowledgements
The Publishers would like to thank the following for permission to reproduce photographs.

Rex Features London: p.5 (top); Clive Barda/P.A.L.: p.5 (bottom), p.12, p.16, p.18, p.19;
Tony Stone Images/J Sneezby/B Wilkins: p.7; Tony Stone Images: p.8, p.11, p.14; Jonathan
Fisher/P.A.L.: p.13; Colin Willoughby/P.A.L.: p.15, p.17; The Bridgeman Art Library: p.20;
Hulton-Deutsch Collection: p.22; Barnaby's Picture Library: p.23, p.24; Rachel
Hughes/P.A.L.: p.26; Pictorial Press Limited: p.28

Cover photograph reproduced with the permission of The Performing Arts Library.

Our thanks to Jim Drake for his comments in the preparation of this book.

Every effort has been made to contact copyright holders of any material reproduced in this
book. Any omissions will be rectified in subsequent printings if notice is given to the
Publisher.

CONTENTS

INTRODUCTION

The modern world is a noisy place. We hear all kinds of sounds, from traffic noise to the softest music. We hear people talking. Many sounds have a special meaning – the sound of a telephone ringing, a fire alarm, a jet aeroplane passing overhead. All these sounds travel through the air as sound waves. Everything we hear is the result of sound waves entering our ears. So what are sound waves?

Waves of sound

When a gong is struck with a hammer, the gong vibrates. While it continues to vibrate, we hear the musical sound the gong makes. The gong's vibration forces the air **molecules** around it to vibrate backwards and forwards. This causes air molecules around the gong either to crowd together or to space out rapidly. Where they crowd together they create regions of high **air pressure**. Where they are spaced out there are regions of low air pressure. These regions spread outwards from the source of the sound, the sounding gong. They are the sound waves which our ears hear.

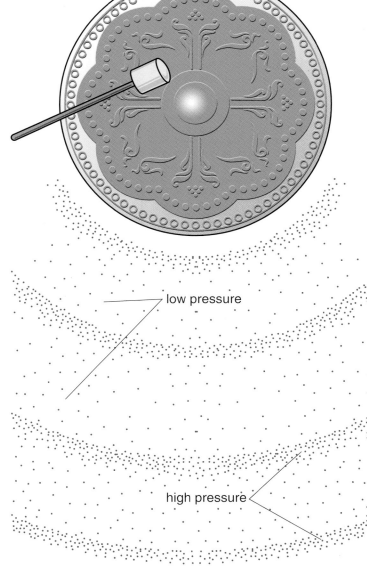

low pressure

high pressure

The distance between one region of high air pressure to the next region of high air pressure is equal to the wavelength of the sound. A low sound has a longer wavelength than a high-pitched sound; a lower sound also has a lower **frequency** – there are fewer complete waves of sound each second.

All sorts of instruments

Music is the arrangement of sounds into patterns that are interesting or pleasing to the listener. If the sounds are not pleasant, the result is noise! People play music for many reasons – for relaxation, for entertainment and to express their feelings. Music – pop, classical or religious – is part of everyone's culture. Music can be as simple as beating out a rhythm on a drum or as complicated as a musical performance involving hundreds of singers and a full orchestra with musicians playing stringed, woodwind, brass and percussion instruments.

With the invention of radio, records and tapes, more people now listen to more music than at any time in history. New sounds and ways of making music, using **electronic** instruments and computer techniques, are constantly being explored.

The clear, ringing sound of a steel band is typically Caribbean. The tuned drums are made out of metal oil barrels, cut in half. Shallow, circular depressions are beaten into the flat top or bottom sections of the drums. Each depression plays a different note. The larger drums play the lowest notes of all.

When a soprano sings a high note she can be heard at the back of a large auditorium. The musical sound that a human voice makes is produced by vibrations of parts of the throat called the vocal cords.

YOUR EARS

The familiar sounds you hear all around you travel via air particles into your ears. High sounds, like a whistle, are caused by air particles vibrating very quickly. Low sounds, like a distant rumble of thunder, are caused by slow vibrations in the air. Sound is a form of energy, and your ears are marvellous devices that convert sound energy into sounds that you can hear. How do you hear sound?

Listening

Your ear has three main sections. The outer ear, or auricle, is the part of your ear that you can see. It collects sounds and funnels them down a short tube inside the ear, called the auditory or ear canal.

At the end of the ear canal, about 2.5 cm inside your ear, a membrane (thin sheet of tissue) called the eardrum stretches over the opening to the middle ear. When sound waves hit the eardrum they make it vibrate.

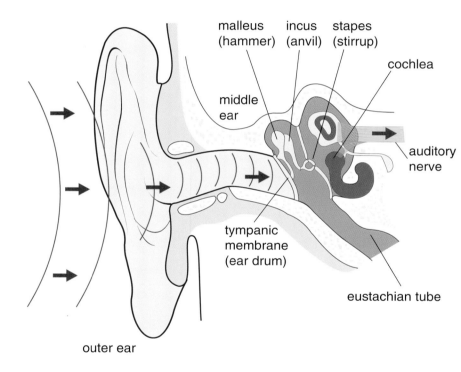

malleus (hammer) incus (anvil) stapes (stirrup)

cochlea

middle ear

auditory nerve

tympanic membrane (ear drum)

eustachian tube

outer ear

These vibrations are picked up by three tiny connecting ear bones called ossicles. (One of them, the stirrup, is the smallest bone in your body.) The ossicles pass these vibrations to the cochlea, a fluid-filled, spiral tube in the inner ear. Inside the inner ear, movements of the fluid cause tiny sensitive hairs to vibrate. Their movement generates electrical signals which the auditory nerve sends to the brain. The brain decodes these signals and you hear a sound.

Sound, or air vibrations being converted into electrical signals in your ear. The same thing happens inside a **microphone!**

High and low notes

The frequency of sound waves is the number of vibrations that a sound makes every second. Scientists use a unit called the **hertz** (Hz) to measure frequency. One hertz (1 Hz) is one complete wave every second. Human beings can hear sounds between 20 Hz (a low rumble) and 20,000 Hz, which is so high that only children can hear it. This is because many adults lose their ability to hear high notes as they get older. Dolphins, however, can hear sounds with a frequency of an astonishing 120,000 Hz. Whales use low-frequency sounds to communicate across vast distances in the oceans.

A dog can hear far higher sounds than we can – which explains why when we see a shepherd blow a special dog whistle we hear nothing, but the dog obviously does!

SOUND AND RADIOWAVES

Two Germans made important discoveries in physics. Herman Helmholtz (1821–94) studied sight and hearing, and showed how the cochlea in the ear works. His pupil, Rudolf Hertz (1857–94), discovered electromagnetic (radio) waves.

SOUND BEHAVIOUR

Do you like singing in the bath? The sounds you make echo off the flat bathroom tiles, and there are no soft furnishings nearby to absorb sound. Nearly anyone can sound like an opera star! But echoes, and materials that absorb sound, can be a problem in a large auditorium, causing some sounds to vanish altogether. It is very difficult to design a concert hall so that all instruments and speech can be clearly heard by everyone in the audience, wherever they are sitting. So how does sound behave?

SPEED OF SOUND

Sound travels through air at a speed of 344 m per second. Fighter planes regularly fly faster than the **speed of sound** through the air (about 1230 km or 760 miles per hour).

The Whispering Gallery in the dome of St Paul's Cathedral, London, is famous because of its **acoustics**. A whisper near the wall on one side can be clearly heard on the other, 32.6 m away. Ordinarily this would be impossible, but the circular shape reflects the smallest sound.

Listening to music

In a Gothic church with a high vaulted ceiling, even small sounds such as whispering will echo and reverberate (echo repeatedly). These effects make music come alive, but if there are too many echoes you can't hear anything clearly. If there are none at all, the music sounds dead. When performers rehearse in empty theatres or concert halls they notice the difference. When there is an audience of listeners present, their clothes and bodies absorb sound, cutting down the reflection of sound.

Making sounds

A musical instrument makes a sound because part of the instrument is vibrating. It could be a string, the skin of a drum, the wooden bar of a xylophone or a moving column of air inside a wind instrument. These vibrations generate sound waves which have the same **frequency** (rate of vibration) as the musical note produced by the instrument. The note to which string players tune their instruments is A, which has a frequency of 440 Hz.

Sound waves can be made visible using an instrument called an oscilloscope. It shows pictures of sound waves on a small TV screen. A very pure note, like that made by a tuning fork, produces a very smooth, regular wave pattern. A gong makes a jagged, irregular pattern, and a violin note makes a complicated but regular pattern.

Sound reflections

Echoes are reflections of sound waves. When you shout loudly, the sound you make travels outwards from you. If it meets a hard, flattish surface, such as the wall of a room, the sound is reflected – it changes direction just like a beam of torchlight on a mirror. If you are out in the open near a building, a wall or in the mountains, you may also hear echoes.

VOICE TRICKS

If people swallow a mouthful of helium from a party balloon and then talk, they will sound like Mickey Mouse! This is because sound travels at different speeds through different substances – gases, liquids and solids – and so distorts.

In the mountains, you can hear your voice echoing back to you when you shout. The sound bounces off a surface such as the face of a cliff, and you may hear several echoes before the sound dies away. Because sound travels at a fixed speed, the time an echo takes to return tells you how far away the cliff face is.

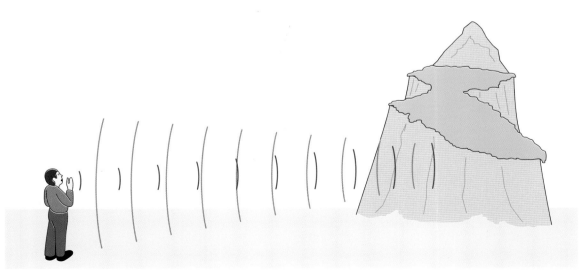

MUSICAL NOTES

Yﾠou must have heard some music and then said afterwards, 'I can't get that tune out of my head.' You remember the melody (tune) and its rhythm. A composer also uses harmony and tone colour and, of course, chooses the notes to make a good piece of music. But how do composers pass onto musicians the sounds or music they have in their heads?

Writing it down: music notation

The ancient Greeks were the first people to make letters stand for musical notes. The system of writing down notes (notation) has changed little since the fourteenth century. The familiar lined music paper was invented much later. In Britain, Australia, Germany and the USA notes are named after the letters A, B, C, D, E, F and G. In Italy and France they are *ut*, *re*, *mi*, etc.

The series of five lines on a musical score is called a stave. It is divided by vertical lines into bars (groups of beats) where the musical notes and rests, are written. The rests show pauses (how long not to play for) and the different designs of notes show how long they should be played for. Where each note appears on the stave tells you which note to play.

PYTHAGORAS' PITCH

People first tried to understand music on a scientific basis a long time ago. For example, Pythagoras, the famous Greek mathematician (c. 582–507 BC), investigated the **pitch** of a note created by a stretched string. The pitch of a note describes how high or low it is. He discovered that pitch depends exactly on the length of the string; the shorter the string, the higher the pitch.

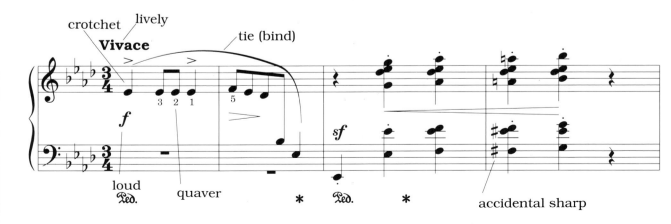

crotchet · lively · Vivace · tie (bind) · loud · quaver · accidental sharp

One piece of music can be divided into different parts for different instruments, so they can all play together in harmony.

Tone colour

A piano sounds quite different from a trumpet. Why is this? There is a special quality of a musical note that helps a listener to tell which instrument is playing. It is called timbre or tone colour. The sound of each instrument has a different timbre. Although the main frequency of the same note on different instruments is the same, each instrument colours every note with characteristic **harmonics**.

MEASURING SOUND

Scientists use a unit called a decibel (dB) to measure the 'loudness' of a sound. The smallest, or least intense, sound that a normal human ear can hear is 0 decibels. In contrast, a jet airliner taking off creates about 120–130 dB, the same as amplified music at a rock concert. The noise of rustling leaves is about 30 dB.

WHISTLES, PIPES AND FLUTES

You can make a musical note by blowing across the neck of a bottle. Like a bottle, most wind instruments consist of a hollow tube, but they also have a mouthpiece. They have been around since ancient times – whistles carved from the toe bones of reindeer 40,000 years ago have been found in France. Wind instruments make sounds when the air inside the hollow tube vibrates.

Whistle a cheerful tune

When you blow into a woodwind instrument, a flute or a whistle, you make the air inside the instrument vibrate. This movement of air produces the note. By covering the holes in the instrument with your fingers, you can change the length of the column of air vibrating inside the flute. This changes the note.

Panpipes produce a haunting, breathy sound and are associated with the mythical Greek god Pan. The deeper notes are made by blowing across the long pipes; the higher pitched ones are produced by blowing across the shorter pipes.

A FAMILY OF INSTRUMENTS

Not all woodwind instruments are made from wood. The modern concert flute is made of metal and makes a bright clear sound. Like the flute, the piccolo is held sideways, but sounds one octave higher. The bright notes of the fife, a small side-blown flute, sound high above the rhythms of a marching band.

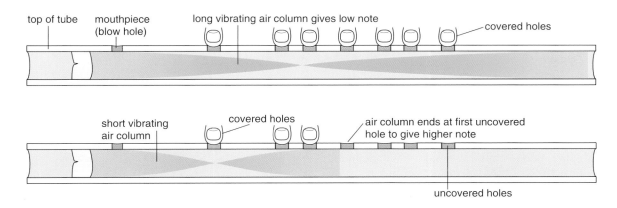

top of tube | mouthpiece (blow hole) | long vibrating air column gives low note | covered holes

short vibrating air column | covered holes | air column ends at first uncovered hole to give higher note

uncovered holes

When a flute player covers all the holes of the flute, the note produced is the lowest possible, because the column of vibrating air is long. When some of the holes are uncovered, a higher note is sounded: the column of vibrating air is now shorter. The same principle is used to change the pitch of the sound in wind instruments such as the oboe, clarinet and bassoon.

FLAUTIST'S FINGERS

Theobald Boehm (1794–1881) set out to make the perfect flute. He was an inventor and a flautist, and soon found that he would have to make holes in places where the flute player's fingers could not reach. So he made the key mechanism that modern flutes still use.

The complex keywork of a modern metal concert flute makes it easier to play than its simple wooden ancestors, and it has a much brighter sound. Some of the pads are closed directly by the flautist's fingers, and others by keys operated by the thumbs or little fingers.

LISTEN TO THE BAND

Brass instruments make a fantastic sound. Most of them have a mouthpiece at one end of a hollow tube and a flared bell at the other. The sound made by the player's lips vibrating against the mouthpiece is the **fundamental** note of the instrument. By changing the tightness of the lips, and blowing harder or softer, the player raises or lowers the pitch of the note. This is the only way to play different notes on a hunting or coach horn.

Blazing fanfares

A fanfare on a trumpet is a blaze of sound that can be clearly heard above any other instrument. The trumpet's hollow tube is coiled, and a system of valves directs air through a shorter or longer length of the instrument.

Sometimes a trumpet player puts a round object called a mute inside the bell of the instrument. A mute does not silence the trumpet. It makes it quieter and gives the sound a special quality. Mutes with different shapes produce a jazzy, buzzy quality, or change the bright, open sound into a thin piercing wail.

All the different brass instruments are played in a military band, as well as clarinets , piccolos, bassoons and a variety of percussion instruments.

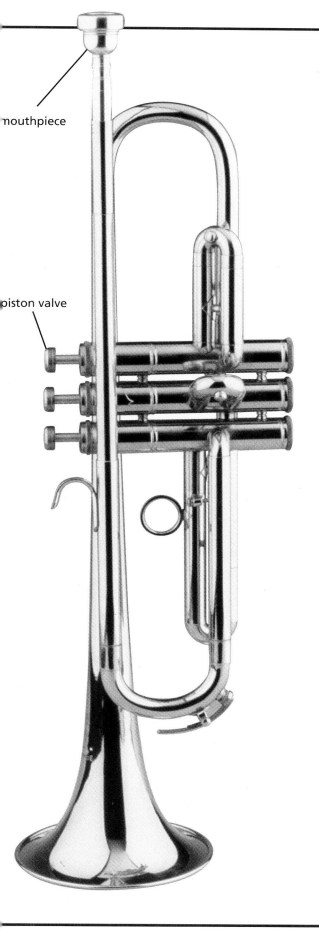

mouthpiece

piston valve

A trumpet has three piston valves which open up or shut off longer passages for the vibrating air. As for all wind instruments, the longer the passage or tube, the lower the note.

THE SAX

The saxophone was patented in 1834, and was used first in military bands before becoming a leading jazz instrument. Although it is a brass instrument it has a very different mouthpiece. Instead of having a fixed brass 'tube' to blow into, the saxophone has a reed – sliver of bamboo – which the player puts inside their mouth. It is the vibrating reed which causes a column of air inside the instrument to vibrate.

PHAROAH'S TRUMPETS

Excavations of the tomb of the Egyptian pharoah Tutankhamen in 1923 revealed that trumpets were buried with him. The instruments were still playable.

THE OLDEST INSTRUMENTS

When you think of percussion instruments you hear the crash of cymbals and the rhythm of drums. There are many different kinds of percussion instrument – in fact anything that makes a sound when you hit it or shake it can be used as a percussion instrument. Maracas, for example, consist of beads or lead shot inside wooden shells or hollow gourds. They are played by shaking the maracas to produce a repetitive rhythm for a group or singer. Percussion instruments are used in folk music all over the world.

Xylophone

Each wooden bar of a xylophone makes a different note. The bars are arranged in the same way as the black and white keys of a piano. The pitch of each note varies with the length of the bar; shorter bars produce higher notes. Their sound is amplified (made louder) by hollow metal tubes hanging underneath, which resonate. **Resonance** happens when one vibrating object, in this case the xylophone bar, causes something else to vibrate.

A vibraphone, like a xylophone, is played by striking the bars. The bars are metal and the beater has a soft head. Metal tubes that contain electric fans are positioned under the instrument and produce a **vibrato** effect.

PERCUSSION IN TUNE?

Xylophones, tubular bells and kettle drums are examples of tuned instruments. African 'talking drums', like the kalengo from Nigeria, can be continually tuned to produce high and low notes. Other instruments, like cymbals, castanets, triangles and some drums, are not tuned to play a particular note.

Evelyn Glennie is the first full time, solo percussionist in the world. A remarkable musician (who is also hearing impaired), she owns more than 700 different percussion instruments collected from all over the world. Here she is performing on the xylophone.

Drums

Drums are played all over the world and they all have the same basic design. The drumhead, the drum's most important part, is made of skin or plastic and is stretched over the hollow body shell of the instrument. Some drums are bowl-shaped like the tympani of an orchestra; others are tube-shaped. Tambourines are a kind of drum with a round open frame. Drums are tuned by adjusting the **tension** of the drumhead. Tension screws or levers at the side of the drum can be tightened to stretch the drumhead more. This raises the drum's pitch. To lower the pitch, the screws or levers are loosened.

A basic drum kit consists of a bass drum, tom-toms, a floor drum (tenor drum), a snare drum and cymbals. Drummers use different beaters – hard-headed and soft-headed sticks and a wire brush. The floor drum is operated by pedals.

KEYBOARDS

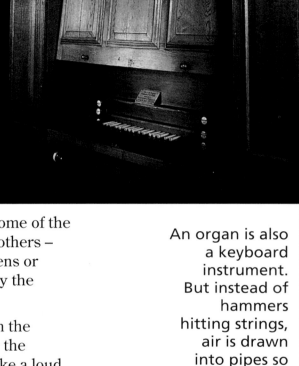

A keyboard is like a set of levers, linking each movement of the player to the production of a note. A piano player sounds a different note with each finger, and can control the loudness of the sounds with soft and loud foot pedals. An electronic keyboard uses electronics to imitate the sound of many different instruments, including a piano.

The piano

If you were to look inside a piano you would see a range of metal strings. The strings are shorter at one side and longer towards the other. If you play a high note, the note you hear is made by a short string; low notes are made by longer strings. Some of the strings are much thicker and heavier than the others – they too have a lower note. A piano tuner tightens or loosens the piano strings until they have exactly the correct pitch.

The characteristic sound of a piano comes from the wooden soundboard which is positioned under the strings. A vibrating string by itself does not make a loud sound, so the vibrating wood of the soundboard helps to reinforce the sound of the strings.

An organ is also a keyboard instrument. But instead of hammers hitting strings, air is drawn into pipes so the air vibrates in them like it does in a flute.

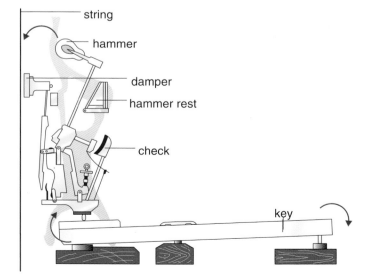

string
hammer
damper
hammer rest
check
key

The piano keys operate felt-covered wooden hammers. These strike the strings. When the keys are at rest, dampers press on the strings to stop them vibrating. The mechanism that links the key to the hammer also raises the damper as the note is played.

monitor

speaker

speaker

sound module

printer

keyboard

home keyboard

If you have the right software, you can compose and play music on the keyboard of a home computer. The computer has to be linked to loudspeakers or a MIDI system. You can even print out your music as a finished music score.

Complete control

A synthesizer is an electronic instrument which can record, reproduce or change virtually any sound possible. It can create actual sounds and store them in its computer. A synthesizer can change the pitch of a note electronically. A system called a MIDI (Musical Instrument Digital Interface) can link together electronic instruments, keyboards and computers.

There are 88 keys on a modern piano, each key plays one note. These notes are a semitone apart from their next neighbour and they are arranged in groups of twelve notes called octaves. You can see the repeated pattern of keys on the keyboard.

ONE, FOUR OR MORE STRINGS

When an archer shoots an arrow, the string of the bow makes a musical twang. At first, lyres were little more than 'musical bows'. Harps have been found by archaeologists looking for traces of the earliest civilizations.

There are two main types of stringed instrument: those like the violin, which are played by drawing a bow across the strings, and those like the harp or guitar, which are played by plucking the strings.

Notes and harmony

Players of a stringed instrument such as a violin, a sitar or a guitar, produce different notes by pressing on a string with their fingers. This changes the string's length. If the string is divided in two, the note will vibrate twice as quickly – it has twice the frequency of the original note. Every note has a different frequency.

LUTES

The lute is an old ancestor of the guitar and violin. Originally from Arabia, it came to Europe in the thirteenth century and is usually pear shaped. There are many different kinds of lute – the South American charango, the Japanese shamisen, the Greek bazouki, the Russian balalaika and the Indian sitar are some of them.

This fifteenth century manuscript painting shows that lutes were played in Europe many centuries ago.

Sounding good

The guitar was already popular all over Europe by the seventeenth century. There are two kinds of modern guitar: the acoustic (or Spanish) guitar and the electric (or rock) guitar. To tune a guitar, the tuning heads are turned to change the tension in the strings. The upper part of the body of a guitar is the soundboard. It is made from two pieces of wood glued together. The soundboard gives the six-stringed acoustic guitar its special sound.

The electric guitar usually has a solid body and devices called pick-ups which are mounted under the strings. These convert the vibrations of the strings into electrical signals. These signals are amplified and heard through a loudspeaker. The strings that play the lower notes are the thickest.

tuning head

pick-up

Violin family members

The violin is the smallest and highest pitched member of the family of stringed instruments. Violas and cellos are bigger and play lower notes. The double bass is by far the biggest stringed instrument, and has the deepest notes. The bow, which consists of a wooden stick with horsehair stretched along its length, is the same shape for all of them. As the player draws the bow across the strings, friction causes them to vibrate.

The body of a violin acts as a resonator, enhancing and amplifying the sound waves from the vibrating strings.

RECORDING MUSIC

Your two ears tell you where a sound is coming from. They give it 'depth'. When you hear music coming from only one loudspeaker it seems flat and uninteresting; it is **monaural**, which is like listening with only one ear. With a **stereophonic** recording the music sounds real when it is replayed. You need two or more microphones to record stereophonic music. So how are the recordings made?

Making a record

Recording consists of making a permanent copy of sound waves. On a record, this copy is stored in the spiral groove on the surface of the record. Examine the groove with a magnifying glass and you will see a pattern of waves. Deep waves produce low sounds; lots of waves mean high sounds. On a tape, the sounds are copied onto bands, or tracks, of magnetism, and on a CD (compact disc), there is a pattern of tiny pits (dents) in the disc.

The first record

Thomas Alva Edison (1847–1931), an American, became famous when, in 1877, he invented the phonograph – the first record player. To make Edison's phonograph work, you turned a handle to rotate the cylinder covered in tin foil, and spoke into the mouthpiece. Inside the mouthpiece was a thin disc of metal, with a metal needle attached to its centre. As sounds made the metal disc vibrate, the needle scratched a pattern on the tin foil. Playback was the reverse process. As you turned the handle, the scratches in the tin foil made the needle vibrate the metal disc, reproducing the sounds.

The first words recorded by Edison on his phonograph were 'halloo, halloo'. The world's first talking machine sold for $18 (£12).

Electric records

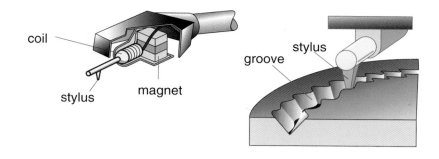

In 1925, a way was found to make and play records electrically. The needle, or stylus, which cut the master record was controlled by an electric current.

The stylus traces the pattern of waves in the groove as the record rotates. The movement of the stylus generates electric signals.

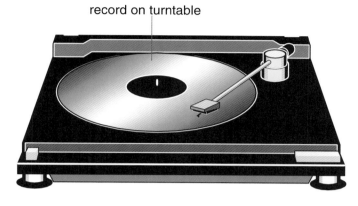

record on turntable

These are amplified (made stronger) electronically, and fed into a loudspeaker. The loudspeaker changes the signals back into sounds.

On a stereo record the stylus traces two sets of sound patterns, or tracks. These are positioned on opposite walls of the groove.

In the recording studio, the different instruments are recorded separately. The sounds are captured by 24 or more microphones on separate tracks. The sound tracks are then 'mixed', to obtain a good balance.
For a stereophonic recording, two tracks are recorded onto one master tape, from which all subsequent tapes, records or CDs are made.

MAGNETIC TAPES

To make a record, a music cassette or a compact disc, a producer first has to record the music on tape. The whole process depends on magnetism and electricity. When an electric current flows in a wire, it behaves like a magnet. If you place a compass near the wire, you will see that the compass needle no longer points in a north–south direction. If you wind a wire around a piece of iron, the iron will become a strong magnet while the electric current flows. Or, if you move a magnet near a coil of wire, an electric current will flow in the wire. This is **electromagnetism** at work. So how does tape recording work?

The microphone

During a recording, the sound is first captured by a microphone. One kind of microphone is the moving-coil microphone. It consists of a thin, round plate of metal attached to a coil of wire. The coil is close to, but does not touch, a small permanent magnet. When a sound makes the metal plate vibrate, the coil of wire moves. The magnet causes an electric current to flow in the coil. The amplified current is used to make the recording on tape.

A battery-powered personal stereo offers high-quality sound while you are on the move. Earphones deliver anything from heavy metal rock to language lessons from the cassette to your ears.

MAKING MAGNETS

You can magnetize a needle by stroking it with a magnet. The magnetic field (which is very strong) creates a magnetic effect in the needle. Before the magnetic effect of an electric current was discovered, all magnets were made in this way.

Recording on tape

Plastic recording tape is coated with a thin layer of magnetic grains. These are made of iron or chromium metal and they are like tiny compass needles. On a blank tape, the magnetism of these grains is completely disordered. When a recording is made, an **electromagnet** arranges the magnetic grains into a pattern. This makes a copy of the recorded sounds as bands of strongly magnetized and less magnetized tape.

Playback

On a stereophonic tape there are two separate magnetic channels, or tracks. In order to hear both tracks, the tape runs past two coils of wire. Each coil is wrapped around a separate iron core. The tiny bands of magnetized tape cause minute electric currents to flow in the coils of wire. These electrical signals are amplified and fed to separate loudspeakers or earphones, which change the signals back into the sounds that you hear.

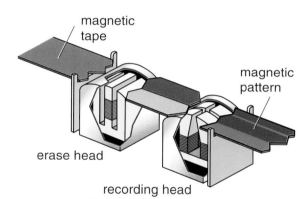

magnetic tape

magnetic pattern

erase head

recording head

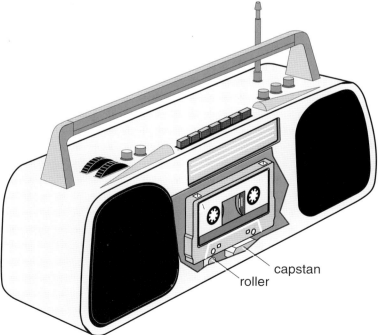

capstan

roller

When the cassette is put into a tape recorder, a motor-driven capstan and a roller keep the tape moving at the right speed over the tape head – an electromagnet which both plays back and records on the tape.

COMPACT DISCS

The music on a compact disc (CD) is recorded by a **laser**. Another tiny laser in the CD player plays back the recorded sounds. How is this done?

A step at a time

When a CD is made, the smooth sound wave is 'measured', 44,100 times per second, and each part of it is given a precise number. Because each part of the sound wave is represented precisely by a number, it can be accurately recorded. This is a **digital** recording. A digital sound recording can be played back without distortion.

A laser makes microscopic pits and flat areas on the surface of the CD which correspond to the sound wave measurements. The depth of each pit is about one-hundredth of the width of a human hair. A CD has at least 3 billion tiny pits.

A master disc made in this way is used to make a stamp, from which all the other discs are manufactured.

On each 12 cm CD there is a spiral track 5 km long that can record more than one hour of music.

Light music

Inside the CD player, a laser reads the 'numbers' at a rate of about 20,000 per second. A beam of light from the tiny laser in the CD player is focused onto the surface of the disc. As the beam strikes the pits and flats on the disc, it is reflected back as a series of pulses of light. These pulses are converted into electrical signals. The signals are amplified and then converted into sounds which you hear through a loudspeaker. Because light from a laser is used to play back CDs (they are not touched by a stylus), they last much longer than **vinyl** records.

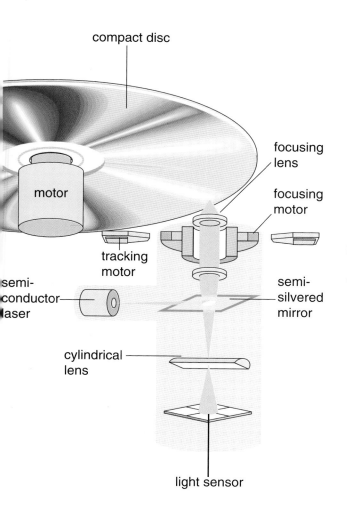

compact disc

motor

focusing lens

focusing motor

tracking motor

semi-conductor laser

semi-silvered mirror

cylindrical lens

light sensor

SOUNDS, WORDS AND PICTURES

A CD stores music in a digital code (pattern of numbers). It can store any other kind of information that can be converted into a digital code; for example one CD can store over 100 million words of text, this is equivalent to more than 100,000 books like this one! More and more computer programs are stored on **CD ROMs**, and the same technique is used to store pictures. Now photographs and also complete movies can be seen and played back using a standard computer. **Multimedia**, which combines pictures, sound and words on a computer screen, would not be possible without the CD!

Two tiny electric motors in a CD player focus and move the beam of laser light that reads the disc. They keep the laser light beam in the right position on the disc all the time. By using four light sensors to detect the exact position of the reflected beam of light, they can quickly refocus and realign the laser.

AT A MUSIC FESTIVAL

A live music concert, with an audience of tens of thousands of people, is much more thrilling than just listening to a recording. A giant array of loudspeakers produces sounds that are loud enough for everyone to hear. The engineers arrange dazzling lighting effects using lasers, and the performers put on a show that everyone remembers long afterwards.

Catching every sound

At a concert, sound engineers carefully position many microphones to pick up the sounds made by the various instruments and performers. When sound waves reach a microphone they cause tiny mechanical movements, which the microphone converts into a pattern of electrical signals. These signals are very weak and they must be made much bigger before they can travel to the loudspeakers.

Sound and light engineers have to co-ordinate every second of the show.

The pattern of electrical signals produced by a microphone accurately represents the sounds it receives. This pattern is made much stronger by an amplifier. Radios, TVs and record, tape and CD players all have amplifiers inside them. The amplifier uses many transistors, which are like tiny electrical switches. Transistors use a weak electrical current to control a big one – this is just what an amplifier does. The weak electrical signals from the microphone control the more powerful ones produced by the amplifier.

Loud enough?

A loudspeaker is a remarkable device that converts electrical signals into sounds. A key part is a coil of fine wire that is attached to a cone inside the loudspeaker. A changing pattern of strong electrical signals from an amplifier is fed into the coil. These signals turn it into a magnet. Because the coil is in the magnetic field of the speaker's permanent magnet, the coil moves. The changing electrical signal from the amplifier causes the loudspeaker cone to move backwards and forwards, making sound waves. Cones of powerful loudspeakers are made from Kevlar, a plastic material which is even stronger than steel.

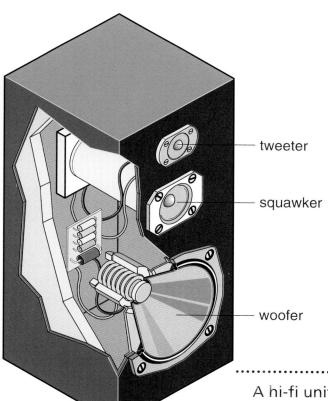

tweeter

squawker

woofer

LASER LIGHT

At a laser light show, bright, narrow beams from lasers move exactly in time to the music. The fantastic patterns of coloured light high above the audience are controlled electronically by the sounds of the music. Because laser light can be so precisely controlled, it has many different uses in science. In industry, powerful lasers cut and drill materials. In medicine, surgical lasers are used for delicate operations such as removing damaged eye tissue. Lasers send vast amounts of information along **fibre-optic cables** which now bring TV, telephone and computer signals directly into our homes.

A hi-fi unit needs three different loudspeakers in the same unit. The deep, low sounds are played through a big loudspeaker called a 'woofer'. The middle range of sound frequencies (500 Hz to 4 kHz) are played by the mid-range unit (squawker). The highest notes (up to 20 kHz) are reproduced by the 'tweeter', which is cone-shaped.

GLOSSARY

acoustics relating to the sense or organs of hearing, to sound, or to the science of sounds

air pressure pressure is the ratio of force to area – a car tyre, for example, is inflated to an air pressure measured in pounds per square inch. In science, air pressure is the force exerted by air on a unit surface, usually a square metre.

CD ROM a compact disc (CD) used to store computer programs, music, pictures or words

digital refers to a device that measures the amount of something in fixed units and jumps from one value to the next, like a digital watch

electromagnet a magnet which consists of an iron core with a coil of insulated wire wrapped around it. It only becomes a magnet when an electric current flows in the wire.

electromagnetism the magnetic effects, for example, of an electric current flowing in a wire

electronic description of anything that depends on the movement of electrons (negative particles of electricity)

fibre-optic cable (or optical fibre) a finely spun thread of glass through which light can be transmitted. Lasers flash coded messages of light that carry vast amounts of information through the optical fibres.

frequency the rate at which something regular is repeated. The number of cycles that a sound wave makes every second. You tune a radio to a station that broadcasts on a certain frequency.

fundamental in music, the first harmonic, such as a note played on a violin, or blown on a trumpet

harmonic a note with a frequency which is a simple multiple of the fundamental note. The upper harmonics give an instrument its characteristic sound.

Hertz (Hz) the unit of frequency, named after Rudolf Hertz. It is used to measure the number of waves of a note that occur each second. Middle C has a frequency of 256 Hz.

laser a device that produces a highly controllable, intense beam of light of one colour

microphone a device for converting sound waves into electrical signals. It is usually connected to an amplifier which, in turn, is connected to a loudspeaker, a tape recorder or a radio.

molecule the smallest amount of any substance that can take part in a chemical reaction

monaural describes musical recordings made before stereophonic recording was possible. There was only one sound track on the recording.

pitch the property of a note that makes you think it is a high or a low note or somewhere in between

resonance forced vibration of an object by a regular driving force, such as vibrations from another object

speed of sound the speed with which sound travels through a gas, a liquid or a solid. It is slowest in gases, and fastest in solids.

stereophonic describes a musical recording made with two or more sound tracks. The sound has depth and you can tell where each sound is coming from.

tension the tightness of the string of a stringed instrument or the drumhead of a drum. The tension is adjusted in order to tune the instrument.

vibrato deliberate repeated changing of the pitch of a note. This gives the note emphasis

vinyl a plastic material from which the first long-playing records were made. It is supposedly unbreakable.

FACT FILE

- The overture '1812', composed by Tchaikovsky, celebrates the retreat of Napoleon's army from Moscow. Near the end of the piece, real cannons are sometimes fired in time to the music. Usually, however, the orchestra makes do with drums and cymbals.

- Church bells in England are rung according to mathematical rules. These make sure that the order in which they are rung is always different. One peal (set) of eight bells has been rung for 40,320 changes without making an error.

- The chanting by the irrigation workers in Egypt who operate the shaduf – the bucket on a stick that lifts water from the Nile – is thought to be the oldest song in the world.

- The metronome was invented by a friend of Ludwig van Beethoven called Johann Maelzel in 1816. Its ticking sound creates an exact tempo (time) for a musician to follow.

- Akio Morita, the president of Sony, is a keen golfer and music lover. He wanted a lightweight, compact device so he could pursue both hobbies at the same time, and so in 1979 the Walkman was invented. Millions have been sold since.

INDEX